To:

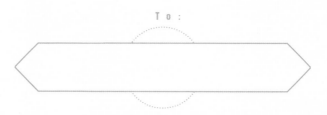

From

The LORD will guide you always;

he will satisfy your needs

in a sun-scorched land

and will strengthen your frame.

You will be like a well-watered garden,

like a spring whose waters

never fail. ISAIAH 58:11

You, God, & Real Life
ISBN 0-310-98546-3
Copyright 2001 by Zondervan

Requests for information should be addressed to:
Inspirio, The gift group of Zondervan
Grand Rapids, Michigan 49530
http://www.inspiriogifts.com

Associate Editor: Molly C. Detweiler
Compilers: Lee Stuart and Emily Klotz
Design Manager: Amy E. Langeler
Book design: Kevin Keller | designconcepts

Printed in China

02 03 04/HK/ 4 3 2 1

YOU, GOD, & REAL LIFE

inspirio™

table of contents

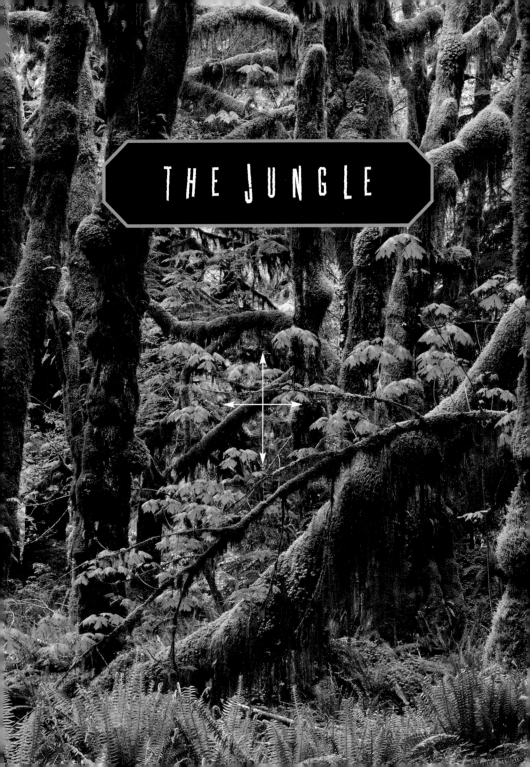

THE JUNGLE

Beginning the Adventure
of the Rest of Your Life

The jungle is a deep, dark, tangled place, bursting with beauty but dense with danger. It takes courage, knowledge, and experience—and in most cases, a guide—to penetrate it and clear a path toward the many treasures it conceals.

Your life ahead right now probably looks a lot like a jungle. As you enter it, you feel excited, eager, and possibly a little lost. You don't know whether you have chosen the right trail, if you have the right tools and gear, or if the promised rewards really exist.

As you enter the jungle, you need to be wary. There are many treasures to be found there, but only one great treasure—God's best for your life—is really worth seeking. To find that best you must choose the right path by following God's leading. You have to be prepared to encounter the poisonous snake called greed. You need to sharpen your tools—your knowledge of God—to hack your way through the underbrush of confusion.

But God himself is our guide through the jungle. He has provided us with a guidebook, his Word. He has promised to lead us past the dangers of a world that honors what is worthless and into his salvation—that's Real Life.

Seeking God's Best for Your Life

> We fix our eyes not on what is seen, but on what is unseen. For what is seen is temporary, but what is unseen is eternal.
>
> 2 CORINTHIANS 4:18

I t's ironic that people tend to put more effort into planning a two-week vacation than they do in thinking about the destiny of their earthly journey. Few people can articulate a clear purpose statement for their lives. Our purpose in life needs to be directed toward God and his kingdom.

Life gets confusing and conflicting. We have to decide what matters most or we become victims of the loudest or latest demands. We have the ability to discern not only the difference between the good and the bad, but also the difference between the good and the best. Since we cannot do everything well, we must carefully choose a few things on which we will concentrate. Ultimately, our purpose for living should be to bring honor to God rather than to bring pleasure to ourselves. With that purpose in mind we can set our priorities by discovering what will bring the greatest recognition to God. If we do that, we'll be rich in God's eyes.

I consider my life worth nothing to me, if only I may finish the race and complete the task the Lord Jesus has given me—the task of testifying to the gospel of God's grace.
ACTS 20:24

Jesus said, "Be faithful...and I will give you the crown of life."
REVELATION 2:10

MAKING DECISIONS WITH GOD'S HELP

"I will instruct you and teach you in the way you should go; I will counsel you and watch over you," says the Lord.

PSALM 32:8

I was facing one of those momentous decision-making times. Having just finished my undergraduate degree, I needed to decide my next course of action. The number of options was staggering. Should I pursue graduate studies, or possibly get further spiritual and ministry training? Should I follow the "guy of my heart" and get married? Should I go overseas on a short-term mission project? Should I try to find a job? I felt that whatever choice I made would radically affect the rest of my life. I didn't know what to do.

Hoping to make the process easier, I tried to involve God. I prayed and read my Bible, but I still felt paralyzed with fear. As I tried to figure out why, I realized that in my heart I really didn't trust God to answer me. I'd always pictured him as a kind of "Big Brother," watching over me not with eyes of love but eyes of judgment, waiting for me to make mistakes or choose the wrong path.

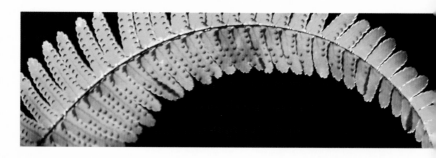

Then I came across Isaiah 30:21: "Whether you turn to the right or to the left, your ears will hear a voice behind you, saying, 'This is the way; walk in it.'" I was amazed. God is not watching me from far away, waiting for me to mess up. No, he is right here with me as I make decisions. He is so concerned for me that he will correct me if a take a wrong turn or get off the path. But I have to know his Word, listen for his voice, and have a heart to obey it—no matter what! TINA LARSON

WHEN YOU START TO WORK IN THE WORLD,
YOU START TO MAKE MONEY, AND WITH MONEY
COMES NEW DECISIONS AND RESPONSIBILITIES.
WHAT DOES THE GUIDE BOOK SAY ABOUT MONEY
AND AVOIDING THE POISON SNAKE OF GREED?

Keep your lives free from the love of money
and be content with what you have,
because God has said: "Never will I leave you;
never will I forsake you."
HEBREWS 13:5

Command those who are rich in this present world not to be arrogant nor to put their hope in wealth, which is so uncertain, but to put their hope in God, who richly provides us with everything for our enjoyment. Command them to do good, to be rich in good deeds, and to be generous and willing to share. In this way they will lay up treasure for themselves as a firm foundation for the coming age, so that they may take hold of the life that is truly life.

I TIMOTHY 6:17–19

Jesus said, "Do not store up for yourselves treasures on earth, where moth and rust destroy, and where thieves break in and steal. But store up for yourselves treasures in heaven, where moth and rust do not destroy, and where thieves do not break in and steal. For where your treasure is, there your heart will be also."

MATTHEW 6:19–21

Whoever loves money never has money enough;
Whoever loves wealth is never satisfied with his income.

ECCLESIASTES 5:10

FINDING YOUR WAY THROUGH CONFUSION

The Lord lifted me
out of the slimy pit,
out of the mud
and the mire;
He set my feet on
a rock and gave me
a firm place to stand.

PSALM 40:2

W hen you have lost the trail...

when the underbrush has obscured the way, depend on your Guide whose vision for your future is ever clear.

Remember, God is the best guide you can have in the jungle. You'll never be lost with God by your side.

When I said, "My foot is slipping," your love, O LORD, supported me.

PSALM 94:18

Don't be fretful about the journey ahead; don't worry about where you are going or how you are going to get there. If you believe in the First Person of the Trinity, God the Father, also believe in the Second Person of the Trinity, the One who came as the Light of the World, not only to die for people, but to light the way. This One, Jesus Christ, is Himself the Light and will guide your footsteps along the way.

EDITH SCHAEFFER

Trust in the LORD with all your heart
        and lean not on your own understanding;
in all your ways acknowledge him,
        and he will make your paths straight.

PROVERBS 3:5—6

MY HOPE IS BUILT ON NOTHING LESS THAN JESUS' BLOOD AND RIGHTEOUSNESS;

I dare not trust the sweetest frame,
but wholly lean on Jesus' name.

> On Christ the solid Rock I stand;
> All other ground is sinking sand,
> All other ground is sinking sand.

When darkness seems to hide His face, I rest on His unchanging grace;
In every high and stormy gale, my anchor holds within the veil.

> On Christ the solid Rock I stand;
> All other ground is sinking sand,
> All other ground is sinking sand.

His oath, His covenant, His blood, support me in the whelming flood;
When all around my soul gives way, He then is all my hope and stay.

> On Christ the solid Rock I stand;
> All other ground is sinking sand,
> All other ground is sinking sand.

When He shall come with trumpet sound, O may I then in Him be found;
Dressed in His righteousness alone, faultless to stand before the throne.

> On Christ the solid Rock I stand;
> All other ground is sinking sand,
> All other ground is sinking sand.

EDWARD MOTE & WILLIAM B. BRADBURY

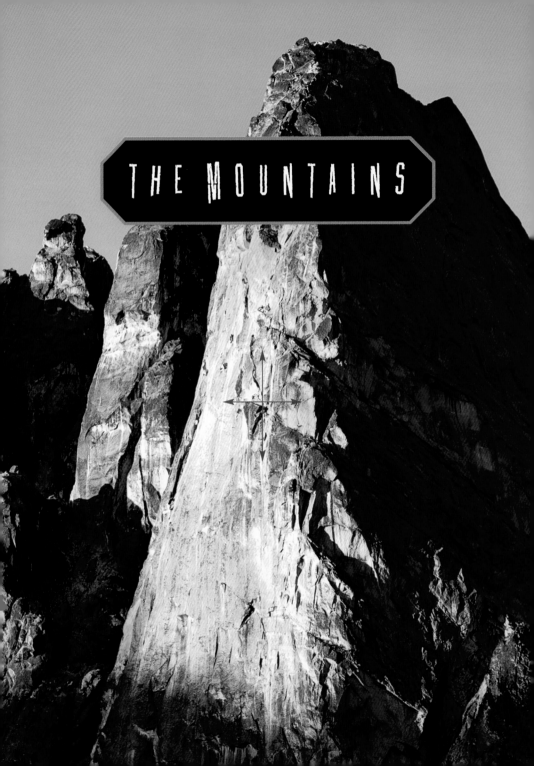

THE MOUNTAINS

Discovering

Joy in the Journey

Mountains have inspired our imaginations and our sense of adventure for centuries. They tower into the clouds, hiding their summits, inspiring many to test themselves by climbing to that mysterious peak. Reaching the summit is a huge achievement, especially considering all the jagged cliffs, frigid winds, and unexpected storms that one encounters along the way. But by putting one hand on the next handhold and one foot on the next step, you can meet the challenge and reach the top. Along the way, there will be much danger, but much beauty. The challenge is to gain the summit while enjoying the journey, allowing God to guide your climb all the way.

The hills are mute: yet how they speak of God!
CHARLES HANDSON TOWNE

TAKING TIME TO LEARN ALONG THE WAY

Come, let us go up
to the mountain
of the LORD....
He will teach us
his ways, so that
we may walk
in his paths.
ISAIAH 2:3

(G) reg could hardly wait to start climbing that mountain.

"Don't rush," his brother cautioned as Greg raced up the trail ahead of them. "You'll miss out if you go too fast. Be careful, you'll ..." But Greg was already far ahead. He was determined to be the first to the top.

"Did you see that eagle? Did you notice those flame red plants and that waterfall?" his companions asked when they finally joined him at the summit. But Greg hadn't seen anything. He didn't even remember passing a waterfall. He began to realize that the whole climb had really gone by in a blur.

He had been too busy racing to the top to notice the climb. He hadn't understood that there is often as much beauty in the climb as there is at the summit.

If you enjoy the journey of your life, you can fully savor the joys of the destination. God is with you and he wants you to be learning along the way. The life of faith is a long, tough climb. But it's filled with beauty, if your eyes are open to see it. There's beauty in every step, in every pause, in every struggle. Strive for the summit, but cherish the process of reaching it.

EDWARD DIDN'T RELISH THE CLIMB.

He didn't like heights and was never good at trail finding.

"Take it slow," he reminded himself, as the others forged ahead. "Enjoy the walk."

At first, Edward was so tense he could barely breathe. He worried about being left behind, getting lost, or being overcome with vertigo. He took a deep breath and noticed a columbine, its singular blue flowers trembling in a rocky crevice.

Then he noticed a chipmunk skittering across the path. A hawk lazed overhead, riding the air currents. Edward walked slowly, taking in all of God's glory, as though seeing it for the first time. He forgot his fears and instead began thanking God for every creature and plant he saw.

The next thing he knew, he was halfway up the mountain and his friends were coming down.

"You'll never make it to the top at the rate you're going," they told him. "And you're really missing out on a panoramic view."

Edward smiled. He had been looking at another amazing view— God's smaller miracles for those who can savor the climb.

Worship the Lord because of his beauty and holiness.

All you people of the earth, tremble when you are with him....

Let the heavens be full of joy. Let the earth be glad

Let the ocean and everything in it roar.

Let the fields and everything in them be glad.

Then all of the trees in the forest will sing with joy.

PSALM 96:9, 11-12 NIRV

EXPECTING THE UNEXPECTED

"When you walk
through the fire,
you will not be burned;
the flames will not
set you ablaze,"
says the LORD.
ISAIAH 43:2

Have you ever been sure of why you were "climbing your mountain" only to find your journey had a much deeper purpose than you first thought? That happened to Doug when he was spending a summer in Indonesia studying the culture. He thought a hike up the volcanic mountain would be a fun break. But the climb turned out to be a "faith test."

"There was a rumbling, then a violent explosion. A softball-sized missile struck me. I was lost in a cloud of swirling, hot, black sand. My friends were nowhere to be seen. I tripped over a hot stone that burned through my shoes. The crater belched again and smoldering rocks pelted the ground. Suddenly, the volcanic cloud lifted and my friends emerged, ash-covered, scorched, supporting each other. John was limping badly. Kristi's right side was scorched and Bruce had ugly burns on his back. How would we make it down the mountain?

"After six hours of hiking, there was still no end in sight. 'God,' I prayed desperately, 'You have to help us down this mountain. We can't do it on our own.' I knew God had already given us the strength to get this far. He was still with us. And we could go on.

"Finally, we met up with some other hikers who helped us the rest of the way down the mountain.

Only later, after we got medical care, did I grasp how close we had been to death. God had protected us when the earth moved and the mountain rumbled. And I knew He would be with me whenever I needed Him again." —DOUG NUENKE

MOUNTAINS COME IN MANY DIFFERENT FORMS—
LIKE MOUNTAINS OF PAPERWORK AND PROJECTS DUE
YESTERDAY OR YOUR HEAP OF A BROKEN-DOWN CAR
WHEN THERE'S NO MONEY TO GET IT FIXED. JUST
WHEN YOU THINK YOU'VE REACHED THE TOP, SOME-
THING UNEXPECTED EXPLODES RIGHT IN YOUR FACE.
YOU'RE CAUGHT OFF GUARD—IT'S IMPOSSIBLE TO
PROTECT YOURSELF FROM THE DELUGE OF LAVA.
YOU CAN EASE THOSE HARROWING MOMENTS WHEN
YOU DRAW ON YOUR FAITH.

GOD WILL HELP YOU FACE WHATEVER COMES YOUR WAY, JUST AS HE DID FOR DOUG.

You are my hiding place, O LORD;
        you will protect me from trouble
and surround me with songs of deliverance. PSALM 32:7

I love you, O LORD, my strength.
        The LORD is my rock, my fortress and my deliverer;
My God is my rock, in whom I take refuge. PSALM 18:1—2

BLESSINGS IN DISGUISE

The Lord heals the brokenhearted and binds up their wounds.
PSALM 147:3

M elanie was determined to climb to to the top. "I'm going to conquer this mountain even if it breaks me," she vowed. She didn't pace herself or take any rest stops. She relentlessly pressed on—and broke down only a half-hour from the top. But in times of brokenness, believes Dr. Charles Stanley, we receive a great gift.

"One of the things I have discovered through being broken is that after brokenness we can experience God's greatest blessings. After brokenness, our lives can be the most fruitful and have the most purpose. The dawn after a very dark and storm-wreaked night is glorious. Feeling joy again after a period of intense mourning can be ecstatic. A blessing can come in the wake of being broken. But this blessing comes only if we experience brokenness fully and confront why it is that God has allowed us to be broken. If we allow God to do his complete work in us, blessing will follow brokenness." CHARLES STANLEY

Remember, every stumble, every "wrong trail," every sore muscle is a gift from God ... if you choose to see it that way. Struggles and failures are sometimes the best way to learn and eventually reach success.

I lift up my eyes to the hills—Where does my help come from?
My help comes from the LORD, The Maker of heaven and earth.
PSALM 121:1-2

29

LETTING GO AND LETTING GOD

"My thoughts are not your thoughts, neither are your ways my ways," declares the LORD. "As the heavens are higher than the earth, so are my ways higher than your ways and my thoughts than your thoughts." ISAIAH 55:8—9

(A)nnie forgot to factor in the long climb down. She thought once she'd reached the summit of the mountain, it was literally "downhill" from there.

But this mountain was different. Going down proved more challenging than climbing up. The trail was full of loose rocks, and she was constantly sliding and falling. She had to test every step. It was getting dark and Annie was tired and discouraged. She was bruised from her stumbles and angry that an experienced climber like herself was going through this. She struggled to stay in control. Then she watched some rocks tumbling down the mountain. God was giving her a hint; there are many ways to follow a trail and just one of them is standing up. She realized if she would let go of her rigidity and frustration, she could take an easier way down.

Cautiously, she sat down and gave herself a little push with her hands. She slid a little way. It felt fun, like sledding as a kid. Annie slid her way down that mountain and slid herself closer to God. By giving up control she was able to follow God on an easier path than her own.

Have you ever climbed part way up a mountain and started sliding down? Suddenly, the earth and rocks that seemed so firm are on the move. Every step forward causes you to lose your footing and scoot backward. You worked hard to get as high as you did and it's frustrating to be falling back toward the bottom.

But there's nothing wrong with walking the same mountain path more than once. You're sure to notice new things. You're sure to feel more confident on your journey.

Think about areas in your life that make you feel like you're sliding backward. What do you think God is trying to teach you?

When you walk with God, it doesn't matter if you're climbing up or sliding down—you will have equal growth in either direction. You will grow strong and brave and confident from your climb. And you will learn that allowing God control of your life makes the journey even more worthwhile.

IF THE LORD DELIGHTS IN A MAN'S WAY,

He makes his steps firm;
Though he stumble, he will not fall,
For the LORD upholds him with his hand.

PSALM 37:23—24

Cast your cares on the LORD and he will sustain you;
he will never let the righteous fall. PSALM 55:22

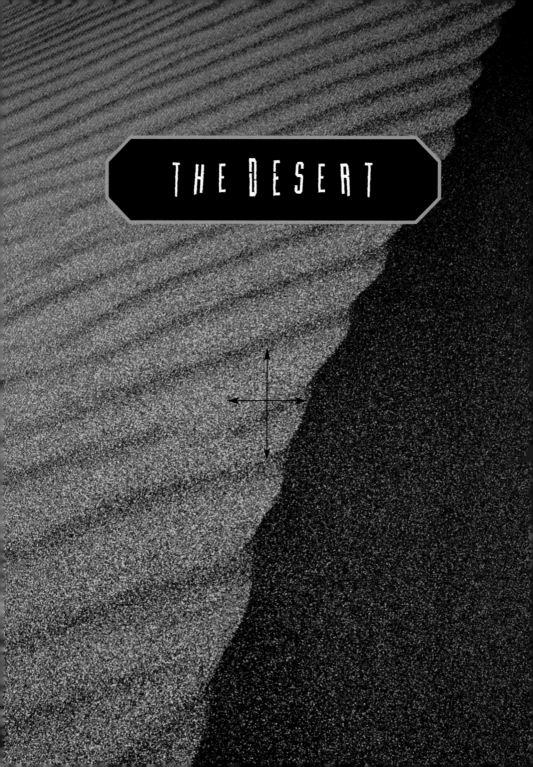

THE DESERT

Finding Living Water
in the Dry Times

The desert wilderness is a climate of extremes—intense heat during sunlight hours and frigid temperatures at night. Rain is a rare occurrence, so water is a scarce and precious commodity. It takes courage and endurance to traverse a desert, especially when there aren't any good maps and no obvious paths to follow.

When you encounter desert times of difficulty in your life, you may feel lost, lonely, and afraid. You may even wonder if you'll be able to make it to the other side and happier times. But we all have to cross deserts in life. We have to survive sandstorms of poor physical and emotional health. We have to resist the temptation to run toward the mirages of unholy promises. And we have to seek shelter when we are in the heat of making hard choices.

But when you are in the desert, you can find relief in the oasis of God's love, the cool, forgiving, refreshing promises of His grace and help. Only when you stop often at his oasis will your journey through the desert be bearable.

LEARNING TO LOOK TO GOD

Teach me to do your will, for you are my God; may your good Spirit lead me on level ground. For your name's sake, O LORD, preserve my life; in your righteousness, bring me out of trouble.

PSALM 143:10—11

Sometimes, despite our best intentions, we find ourselves wandering in a wilderness of anxiety, lost and unable to find our way out. I know. For years I felt that way. Nothing seemed to work; I felt stripped and anxious, unable to determine what my mission in life should be. What was I aiming for? Where was a map out of this hazy land in which I wandered but couldn't find the path out? It wasn't that I hadn't set goals. It's that I didn't know how to set my sights on God and let him lead me where to go.

You may be in the wilderness ... anxiously wandering around, feeling aimless and without a map, fearful disaster is headed toward you. Relinquish your anxieties to God. For he cares for you. THELMA WELLS

There is no shelter in the desert,
  no shade to cool the spirit heated by uncertainty,
  no warmth to ward off the chill of the lost soul's night.
There is only sky and sand,
  a vast void, a limitless land of pain and struggle.
Only the tough survive—
  those who see the blue-white desert sky as God's eternal
  realm,
  those who see the glistening sand as God's grace
    broken into a billion beautiful pebbles,
  those who take shelter in his Word.

HIDING IN GOD'S ARMS

> God is our refuge
> and strength,
> an ever-present help
> in trouble.
> PSALM 46:1

S andstorms (sand-laden winds) occur frequently in most deserts. The "Seistan" desert wind in Iran and Afghanistan blows constantly for up to 120 days. Within Saudi Arabia, sandstorm winds can reach 70 to 80 mph.

According to the Air Cavalry's Desert Survival website, the greatest danger in a sandstorm is getting lost in a swirling wall of sand. If natural shelter is unavailable, it advises that you mark your direction of travel, lie down, and sit out the storm.

We all endure the sandstorms of life—the frenzied, pelting, blinding storms of broken relationships, lost opportunities, and bad choices. Sometimes our storms are physical challenges, when our health and well-being are tossed for a time. Sometimes we confront emotional challenges—with our friends, our family, our schools, our jobs—when every "normal" part of life is blown off course.

In these times, you must be still, lay close to God, and listen to his heart. He may be using this storm to make you stronger.

First Samuel chronicles David's long odyssey from a young shepherd boy into a war hero, a frightened fugitive to a veteran leader and warrior. Would David have become the man he did apart from his many years of heart-breaking exile? What if Saul had stepped aside and immediately yielded the throne to David? We can be sure of one thing: We would not have the same collection of psalms that we treasure today. So many of those songs of trust and appeals for deliverance grew directly out of those running, hiding years.

While in exile in the desert of Judah, he penned words that have encouraged God's people in "dry times" ever since: "O God, you are my God, earnestly I see you; my soul thirsts for you, my body longs for you, in a dry and weary land where there is no water. ... Because your love is better than life, my lips will glorify you (Psalm 63:1, 3).

And what of our walk with God? It may be that our darkest hours and most excruciating experiences will teach us most about our Lord's sufficiency and tender care. Our praise, rising out of such trying hours, may encourage the hearts of many and bring eternal praise to God's name.

FROM THE NIV ENCOURAGEMENT BIBLE

Mirages: Avoiding False Promises

In the desert of difficult times, it's common to see mirages ... ethereal images of oases that promise respite, rejuvenation, even salvation. But mirages are dangerous. The false promises of drugs, alcohol, sex, and money appear before you, beckoning you. They offer you good times, cheap thrills and an escape from having to make difficult choices.

But when you go after them their promises disappear—evaporate. You end up off the trail and even more parched than you were before. Only God offers an oasis that is always and forever real and refreshing.

The world and its desires pass away, but the man who does the will of God lives forever.

1 JOHN 2:17

As we proceed down life's journey, we can choose between two roads: the road of this world's wisdom and the road of God's wisdom. The first leads us through deserts, wastelands, and jagged mountains of perplexity and frustration. By contrast, the wisdom of God takes us through the oasis of understanding and the valley of delight, leading us confidently to fulfillment in this life and the blessings of eternity.   TIM LAHAYE

DIFFICULT CHOICES CAN SEEM LIKE THE UNRELENTING DESERT HEAT. MANY TIMES THESE CHOICES MEAN MAKING SACRIFICES AND FACING HARD TIMES AHEAD, EVEN THOUGH THE CHOICE IS THE RIGHT ONE. IN THESE TIMES OF DECISION, GOD WILL GUIDE YOU TO THE RIGHT PATH—THE ONE THAT WILL EVENTUALLY LEAD TO COOL SHELTER.

Debbi considered herself to be a good Christian. She didn't smoke, swear, or do drugs. And she drank only occasionally. For nearly three years she'd dated Rob, a wonderful Christian boy. Though they had numerous opportunities to make love, Debbi and Rob chose to maintain their virginity. They were proud about their determination to remain pure, though they sometimes joked about being added to the endangered species list.

Midway through her senior year, the unthinkable happened. Debbi spent the night at a friend's house, got really drunk, and had sex with her friend's older brother. Almost immediately she knew she was pregnant, and her world fell apart.

What could she do? An abortion, which she considered to be murder, was out of the question. And she'd probably get killed herself if she talked to her parents. As for Rob, if he found out their relationship would be over. The only way out, she figured, was to trap Rob into having sex so he'd think the baby was his. A quiet marriage could then be arranged.

But deep down, Debbi knew the solution she was toying with would end in disaster. King David was lesson enough. When he'd tried to hush up his shenanigans with Bathsheba by having her husband killed, he didn't get rid of his problem. He merely compounded it. And it wasn't long before he was a miserable, broken man. Sure, Rob could be seduced. He'd probably even marry her. But what would happen later, when he discovered he'd been duped?

In the end, Debbi risked everything and did what she knew was right. She came clean. It was the hardest, bravest thing she ever did, but she felt the Lord assuring her with the words from Isaiah 41:9-10: "I have … not rejected you. So do not fear, for I am with you; do not be dismayed, for I am your God."

Though Rob called it quits, her friends and family rallied to help her through the crisis. And when Debbi's baby girl arrived, a loving Christian couple adopted her with open arms. Seeing their tears of joy didn't exactly make it all worthwhile, but they did help Debbi know she'd made the right decision.

When I think of Debbi, old-fashioned words like intestinal fortitude, and guts, and strength of character come to mind. Yes, she'd made a big, stupid mistake. But I think our mistakes, in God's eyes, are less important than our response to them. Debbi didn't run; she stood firm. And the Lord stood beside her.

S. RICKLY CHRISTIAN

Since we have a great high priest who has gone through the heavens,
Jesus the Son of God, let us hold firmly to the faith we profess.
For we do not have a high priest who is unable to sympathize with our weaknesses,
but we have one who has been tempted in every way, just as we are—
yet was without sin. HEBREWS 4:14-15

It is God who makes ... you stand firm in Christ. 2 CORINTHIANS 1:21

FINDING THE LIVING WATER

"I will refresh the weary and satisfy the faint," says the Lord.
JEREMIAH 31:25

W hen you're wandering in the desert, your thirst can become unbearable. You may become faint, disoriented. But you can find refreshment and strength in faith.

Jacob's well was there, and Jesus, tired as he was from the journey, sat down by the well. It was about the sixth hour.

When a Samaritan woman came to draw water, Jesus said to her, "Will you give me a drink?" ...

The Samaritan woman said to him, "You are a Jew and I am a Samaritan woman. How can you ask me for a drink?" (For Jews do not associate with Samaritans.)

Jesus answered her, "If you knew the gift of God and who it is that asks you for a drink, you would have asked him and he would have given you living water."

"Sir," the woman said, "you have nothing to draw with and the well is deep. Where can you get this living water?"...

Jesus answered, "Everyone who drinks this water will be thirsty again, but whoever drinks this water I give him will never thirst. Indeed, the water I give him will become in him a spring of water welling up to eternal life." JOHN 4:6-7, 9-11, 13-14

JESUS SAID

"I AM THE ALPHA AND THE OMEGA, THE BEGINNING AND THE END.

To him who is thirsty I will give to drink without cost
from the spring of the water of life." REVELATION 21:6

Let us acknowledge the LORD;
let us press on to acknowledge him.
As surely as the sun rises, he will appear;
he will come to us like the winter rains,
like the spring rains that water the earth. HOSEA 6:3

The LORD will guide you always;
He will satisfy your needs in a sun-scorched land
and will strengthen your frame.
You will be like a well-watered garden,
like a spring whose waters never fail. ISAIAH 58:11

The Lord turned the desert into pools of water
and the parched ground into flowing springs. PSALM 107:35

Seeking God
in the Everyday

American poet Robert Frost described the woods as "lovely, dark and deep." His poetic description reveals the many personalities of the woodlands. They are indeed lovely, filled with soft shadows, wildflowers and the ever-present song of birds in the trees. In the midst of all that beauty, though, the woods can also be dark and deep. Towering trees block out much of the sunlight, creating a constant feeling of approaching night. One must be careful to follow a compass and a trustworthy guide to avoid becoming hopelessly lost in the maze of trees and foliage. While the forest looks inviting in the bright light of day, it is full of dangers come nightfall. The woods can be a wonderful adventure or a dangerous labyrinth—it's up to you!

Our everyday lives are very much the same. There are lovely days where our journey through life is full of fun and joy. There are also days when the darkness surrounds us, and we're unsure of our next step. It is especially important on these days to look to God as your guide and to his Word as your compass.

STARTING EACH DAY WITH GOD

In the morning, O LORD, you hear my voice; in the morning I lay my requests before you and wait in expectation.

PSALM 5:3

For physical and spiritual regeneration, I walk on a path close to my home in the early morning hours. When the alarm rings at 6:00 a.m., I immediately begin finding excuses not to go. I drag myself out of bed because I have made a covenant to meet a friend and walk three days a week. I can't leave her there to walk alone!

The path we walk is a path through the woods. We always carry a book to our favorite place in the woods. (It is also, conveniently, the place where we have to stop to breathe!) We stop, catch our breath, sit under the trees and share a chapter from the Bible, a poem, or a favorite prayer. We are regenerated. The day is redeemed.

Every day of our lives we make choices about how we're going to live. Wherever we find ourselves in this fragile existence, we need to be reminded that life can be brighter than noonday and darkness like morning because we are living fully in this moment, secure in our hope in the Lord.

COURAGE TO FOLLOW WHERE GOD LEADS

Faith in God is
dangerous thinking.
Even more,
faith in God is
dangerous living.
LEONARD SWEET

I was fourteen and I didn't care HOW beautiful it was in the Pacific Northwest. I only had Daddy's word for it that it was beautiful, and it really didn't matter, anyway! I wanted to stay in Missouri and finish high school with my friends. But Daddy felt called to follow God to a pastorate in Portland, Oregon, and it was obvious I was going to be stuck with his decision. I screamed, I begged, I threatened to stay behind and live with my best friend. My parents said, "Trust God and he will help you be strong enough to find friends in your new high school."

That was my first experience jumping off a cliff into a new world. I stepped off with one hand over my eyes and the other firmly hanging on to the familiarity of my past.

Entrusting God with our future can be terrifying. We don't know what he holds in store for us or what path he will lead us down. But consider this: A future NOT trusting God isn't a walk in the park, either! Living by faith in God means trusting him for the unseen and the unknown. That kind of faith is a lifelong process—as we discover we can trust him for each small step along the way, we discover we can trust him for the giant leaps, too. FROM THE COLLEGIATE DEVOTIONAL BIBLE

"THE WOODS WERE FULL OF PERIL—RATTLE-SNAKES AND WATER MOCCASINS AND NESTS OF COPPERHEADS; BOBCATS, BEARS, COYOTES, AND WILD BOAR; LOONY HILLBILLIES, RABIES-CRAZED SKUNKS, MERCILESS FIRE ANTS, POISON IVY, POISON SUMAC, AND POISON SALAMANDERS; EVEN A SCATTERING OF MOOSE LETHALLY DERANGED BY A PARASITIC WORM THAT BURROWS A NEST IN THEIR BRAINS AND BEFUDDLES THEM INTO CHASING HAPLESS HIKERS THROUGH REMOTE, SUNNY MEADOWS AND INTO GLACIAL LAKES."

BILL BRYSON

Does your life sometimes seem like this kind of "walk in the woods?" Does your journey take you headlong into loony hillbillies and crazed moose herds? Maybe that's because of your determination to say, "I did it my way." Listen to this: God declares that it's much better to ask him to show you HIS plan. Be patient. He WILL lead you. FROM THE COLLEGIATE DEVOTIONAL BIBLE

As for God, his way is perfect;
the word of the LORD is flawless.
He is a shield for all who take refuge in him. PSALM 18:30

❖

The highway of the upright avoids evil;
he who guards his way guards his life. PROVERBS 16:17

❖

Even though I walk through the valley of the shadow of death,
I will fear no evil, for you are with me, O Lord. PSALM 23:4

GOD REVEALED IN SIMPLE THINGS

Since the creation of the world God's invisible qualities—his eternal power and divine nature—have been clearly seen, being understood from what has been made.

ROMANS 1:20

I was hiking through the trees after a rain and almost stepped on an earthworm. The worm had actually tied himself in a knot! He was working hard to free himself, and he was making some progress. I chuckled and stopped to help him out of his mess.

I laughed because he reminded me of myself and the situations I sometimes get into in my life. I, too, tie myself in knots hurrying to accomplish things with my own strength, even the work I do for God. I need to let God give me the strength so I don't end up in knots. Spiritual revelations from an earthworm! I thanked God for this gentle reminder from one of his creatures. LEE STUART

The LORD makes springs pour water into the ravines;
it flows between the mountains.
They give water to all the beasts of the field;
the wild donkeys quench their thirst.
The birds of the air nest by the waters;
they sing among the branches.
He waters the mountains from his upper chambers;
the earth is satisfied by the fruit of his work.
He makes grass grow for the cattle,
and plants for man to cultivate—
bringing forth food from the earth:
wine that gladdens the heart of man,
oil to make his face shine,
and bread that sustains his heart.
The trees of the LORD are well watered,
the cedars of Lebanon that he planted.
There the birds make their nests;
the stork has its home in the pine trees.
The high mountains belong to the wild goats;
the crags are a refuge for the coneys.
The moon marks off the seasons,
and the sun knows when to go down.
You bring darkness, it becomes night,
and all the beasts of the forest prowl

The lions roar for their prey
and seek their food from God.
The sun rises, and they steal away;
they return and lie down in their dens. ...
How many are your works, O LORD!
In wisdom you made them all;
the earth is full of your creatures.
There is the sea, vast and spacious,
teeming with creatures beyond number—
living things both large and small.
There the ships go to and fro,
and the leviathan, which you formed to frolic there.
These all look to you
to give them their food at the proper time.
When you give it to them,
they gather it up;
when you open your hand,
they are satisfied with good things. ...
When you send your Spirit,
they are created,
and you renew the face of the earth.
May the glory of the LORD endure forever;
may the LORD rejoice in his works.

PSALM 104:10-22, 24-28, 30-31

A COMPASS NEEDLE ALWAYS POINTS NORTH. FROM IT YOU CAN GET YOUR BEARINGS... EVEN WHEN THE TRAIL ISN'T MARKED AND THE PATH IS HARD TO FOLLOW. IN FACT, IF YOU'RE LOST IN THE WOODS, A COMPASS CAN SAVE YOUR LIFE!

Just as the compass needle points north, the Bible always points to God. When we're lost in the dark paths of life, it points us to the truth, to the light of God's will. Every day we face worries and temptations. We have to make important decisions that will set a course for the rest of our lives.

A compass isn't much good if you don't trust it and follow its direction. Likewise, knowledge of the Bible is great, but if you don't trust it and obey what it says, you'll still be lost in the dark. God's words are different from the words in any other book you'll ever read. The Bible points from the darkness to the light, from death to life! FROM THE COLLEGIATE DEVOTIONAL BIBLE

Are you uncertain about which direction you should go? Take your question to God and receive guidance from either the light of His smile or the cloud of His refusal. You must get alone with Him, where the lights and the darknesses of this world cannot interfere and where the opinions of others cannot reach you. You must also have the courage to wait in silent expectation, even when everyone around you is insisting on an immediate decision or action. If you will do these things the will of God will become clear to you. And you will have a deeper concept of who He is, having more insight into His nature and His heart of love.

DAVID, A SIXTH-CENTURY WELSH SAINT

YOUR WORD, LORD, IS A LAMP TO MY FEET AND A LIGHT FOR MY PATH.

PSALM 119:105

Jesus said, "I am the light of the world.
Whoever follows me will never walk in darkness,
 but will have the light of life." JOHN 8:12

God, who said, "Let light shine out of darkness,"
made his light shine in our hearts to give us the light
of the knowledge of the glory of God in the face of Christ.
2 CORINTHIANS 4:6

THE PRAIRIES

Learning to Wait

As you travel through the prairies and plains, nothing stands out—no fascinating rock formations, no majestic trees, no sparkling lakes. It looks like an expanse of endless, flat land and dried-out weeds.

Perhaps you've gone through periods when your life felt like the prairie looks—flat, weedy and "plain." Everyone else seemed to be speeding past you, more successful, more motivated, and more filled with happiness.

But you can find God's plan in the secret beauty, hidden potential, and unique richness of the plains. Stop and listen. The grasses rustle soothingly. Take time to walk through the "weeds"—underneath the pale brittle stalks, the earth is moist and brimming with wildflowers. Stop and really look—those fields are shades of purple, silver, and blue.

The prairie times in your life are God's way of reminding you to hold on to your dreams, though their realization seems nowhere in sight. When your life seems monotonous, when your dreams seem a distant glimmer, slow down, look around, and notice the small steps you have already taken. It's okay to get dust on your face and to stop to pluck cockleburs off your clothes. When your life seems like a dull, flat endurance walk, look for God on the horizon—and wait.

IF YOU'VE EVER FELT LIKE YOU'RE NEVER GOING TO MAKE IT ACROSS THE WIDE EXPANSE BETWEEN YOU AND YOUR DREAMS OR THAT YOUR DREAMS ARE ROUTINELY DISMISSED, DON'T GIVE UP. THE FOLLOWING EXAMPLES, COURTESY OF NORMAN CHALFIN OF THE PROPULSION LABORATORY'S OFFICE OF PATENT CONTROL, INDICATE THAT YOU'RE IN DISTINGUISHED COMPANY:

▼ When Samuel F. B. Morse asked Congress for a grant to build a telegraph line between Washington, D.C., and Baltimore, he was greeted with derision and suggestions that instead he build "a railroad to the moon."

▼ Asked by Parliament whether the telephone would be of any use in Britain, the chief engineer of the British Post Office answered, "No, sir. The Americans have need of the telephone, but we do not. We have plenty of messenger boys."

▼ H.G. Wells, the visionary British writer, did not think it likely that aeronautics would ever be important in transportation. "Man is not an albatross," he said.

▼ In 1903, a year before the Wright brothers flew at Kitty Hawk, Professor Simon Newcomb, a distinguished astronomer, said that flying without a gas bag was impossible, or at least would require the discovery of a new law of nature.

▼ A week before the Wright brothers' flight, the New York Times editorialized on the rival efforts of Samuel Pierpont Langley, who had just achieved flight by an unmanned heavier-than-air craft: "We hope that Professor Langley will not put his substantial greatness as a scientist in further peril by continuing to waste his time and the money involved in further airship experiments. Life is short and he is capable of services to humanity incomparably greater than trying to fly."

▼ Within three years, the Wrights had an airplane that could fly forty miles an hour for one hundred miles. They offered it to the British navy. The Admiralty declined, explaining that the "aeroplane" would be of no practical use in the naval service.

If it's mediocrity you're after, it can be had easily. But if you are to attain excellence, no matter what the field, you must work with all of your might. You can't be allergic to sweat. You must also, on occasion at least, thumb your nose at the skeptics around you. They've been wrong before and they'll be wrong again.   S. RICKLY CHRISTIAN

Achievements of great worth and importance are not accomplished without patient perseverance and a considerable interval of time. For as the saying goes, "Rome was not built in a day."

E. COBHAM BREWER

You need to persevere so that when you have done the will of God, you will receive what he has promised. For in just a very little while, "He who is coming will come and will not delay."... Now faith is being sure of what we hope for and certain of what we do not see.

HEBREWS 10:36—37, 11:1

Let us not become weary in doing good, for at the proper time we will reap a harvest if we do not give up.

GALATIANS 6:9

"You're Out in Left Field."

That's what Sarah's friends were always telling her, laughing at her ideas. She liked having big ideas; she liked having big dreams. But around her friends, she felt self-conscious. Maybe they were right—why should she expect so much? She wasn't rich, she wasn't all that smart, she didn't have any great connections.

One Saturday she drove out to see her grandma, who still lived alone on her farm at age eighty. The relatives were all worried about Grandma. She was too old to be living way out there by herself, so isolated. Still, Sarah loved the farm. Someone else was growing the crops now, but Grandma knew the status of every field. After they'd had lunch, they settled onto the creaky front porch, and Grandma began discussing each of the fields.

"Way out there, to the east, that's my experimental field," Grandma said. "I'm growing organic out there, sugar peas. The fellows down the road say the bugs will get them all, but I just know they are wrong. I've got gardening skills and I've got God."

As Sarah squinted to see the shimmer of green, she realized those crazy peas were literally way out in Grandma's left field. She felt a smile taking over her face as she looked over all the fields, each beautiful in its own way. She felt God's gentle smile and his quiet voice assuring her that it was okay to have big dreams. Luke 1:37 rang in her heart, "Nothing is impossible with God."

With a new determination in her heart to follow her dreams she lifted her eyes to the blue sky. "Help me hang on to my left field," she prayed.

It's Okay to Be Different

Delight yourself
in the LORD and he
will give you the
desires of your heart.

PSALM 37: 4

Jason had always loved to play the piano. Even though he went into business like his parents urged him to, ("There's no money in music," they said.) playing the piano was one of his passions.

He practiced hard, even though no one was paying him, even though he was not performing. Still, Jason felt the Lord's presence when he played. He felt he was putting on his own best concert, for himself and for God.

Sometimes he joined friends for movies and an evening out, but sometimes he just went home alone, to his music. His mother and sisters worried about him. Too solitary, too anti-social. How would he meet a nice girl? It was easy for Jason to get caught up in their worries.

One morning, after too many evenings out and too many days without music, Jason drove to work a different way. He passed an old vacant field, stubbly and unkempt, in the inner part of the city. Only dandelions, weeds, and thistles were growing in that forgotten field. Suddenly, he saw a glorious shout of yellow.

A single sunflower was blooming triumphantly in the middle of that field. "Outstanding in its field," a voice said in Jason's mind. That sunflower gave Jason the image he needed, the energy to give his worries over to God, and his music as well.

Jason spent the next week searching out a professional piano teacher. He found a classical music and piano performance professor who was giving private lessons. Every week Jason met with the professor to learn more about his true love, music.

One day, after nearly three years of intense practice and dedication to his lessons, Jason's teacher introduced him to the conductor of the local symphony. Their head pianist had just retired and they were looking for someone new. After listening to Jason play through only half of a concerto, the conductor offered Jason the position.

As he took his seat at the beautiful, ebony grand piano for his first performance, the image of that solitary sunflower flashed into Jason's mind. And in his heart, he sent up a silent prayer of thanks to his God for the fulfillment of his dream. God had allowed him to be "outstanding in his field."

LOOKING THROUGH GOD'S EYES

The LORD does not look at the things man looks at. Man looks at the outward appearance, but the LORD looks at the heart.

1 SAMUEL 16:7

o often, our life seems as dull and flat as the prairie. But when we invite God into our lives, we see extra richness and excitement in even the flattest of fields. Things that seemed dull and one-dimensional, such as certain jobs or certain people, are often mysterious and blossoming and full of all different kinds of life—if we're willing to look through God's eyes. God can make the ordinary task of waiting into the extraordinary experience of discovering.

❖

Joy did not want her vacation to end. She hated leaving the glorious mountains and dreaded the long drive home, past endless fields and prairies. She felt nearly hypnotized with boredom as she drove across the long, flat stretch of prairie. Suddenly she was brought back to reality when her car sputtered and stopped. Steam poured out of the hood. She was stuck. Using her cell phone, she called a towing service.

After waiting for a half hour, she decided to a stroll through the prairie. The grasses rustled soothingly. Underfoot, the earth was moist and dotted with yellow and orange wildflowers. The fields were shades of purple, silver and blue. Out of the wide expanse of blue above her, a red-winged blackbird soared and landed on a tall blade of prairie grass. A few feet away, Joy suddenly noticed a small lizard, sunning itself on a large boulder that was nestled in the grasses. Joy smiled and actually began to feel glad about her car breakdown!

From a distance, the prairie had seemed boring. But now, Joy discovered a unique beauty she never knew existed. So you see, things aren't always as they seem.

Jesus told [his disciples] a parable:
"The kingdom of heaven is like a mustard seed, which a man took and planted in his field. Though it is the smallest of all your seeds, yet when it grows, it is the largest of garden plants and becomes a tree, so that the birds of the air come and perch in its branches."
MATTHEW: 13:31—32

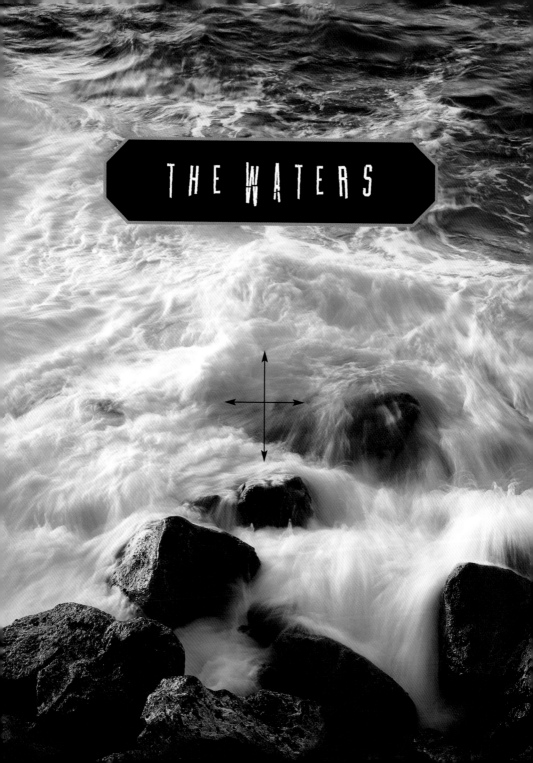

THE WATERS

Life and Depth Experiences

Water—without it, nothing could live, no plants, no animals, no people—nothing. Humans can go sixty days without solid food, but can only go without water for about three days. Water is a wonderful gift God gave to our planet.

Water can also be very frightening, especially in large quantities. It sometimes takes a lot of courage to take that first leap off of the diving board or that first step out of the boat. But once we take that leap and learn to swim, we find a wonderful freedom in enjoying the depths.

❖

Being from the Midwest, Jeff wasn't used to swimming in the ocean. He found the experience both thrilling and nerve-wracking. When a wave pushed Jeff into deeper water, he panicked. All he could think of was the old "JAWS" movie. The more he struggled, the more water he got in his mouth, the more afraid he became.

Jeff didn't realize that God had given him everything he needed to flourish in deep water. If he simply leaned his head back in the water and stretched out, his body would naturally float. Have you ever found yourself in deep water and forgotten your ability to float? God doesn't put you in over your head so you'll drown—God wants you to let go of your fears and dive into your faith.

WATER HAS MANY WAYS TO CARRY YOU FORWARD, IF YOU PAY ATTENTION TO ITS MAJESTIC POWERS AND MYSTERIES. IT'S OKAY TO FLOUNDER, GET WATER IN YOUR MOUTH, OR PUSH YOUR WAY OFF THE BOTTOM. BEING IN OVER YOUR HEAD MEANS HAVING THE COURAGE TO TREAD INTO THE UNKNOWN. THE DEEPER YOU GO, THE DEEPER YOUR CONNECTION TO GOD.

YOU DON'T HAVE TO BE A GREAT SWIMMER OR SAILOR: THE SECRET TO GETTING CLOSER TO GOD IS BEING WILLING TO JUMP IN.

God generally helps people's faith grow by asking them to take the first step. When God called Moses to get out of the boat—to confront Pharaoh and lead his people—Moses balked. So God asked him to take a small step. "Throw down your staff." Moses did and immediately it became a serpent. Serpents were worshiped in Egypt and were regarded as poisonous, so Moses would have been struck by the next command, "Put out your hand and pick it up—by the tail." Moses picked up the snake and it became a staff again. Moses discovered God was faithful. But Moses had to pick it up first. He had to take a first step. God promised Moses and the Israelites freedom. He did deliver them from Pharaoh, but first they had to act in trust. They had to march to the Red Sea before he parted it. JOHN ORTBERG

Imagine marching up to the Red Sea—would you feel fear, doubt, exultation? Even though the miracle of the Red Sea happened thousands of years ago, God "parts the waves" for you every day. Your Red Sea might be a job interview, a date, or an exam. Just remember when you walk into those deep and dangerous situations with God, you may realize that you are really walking on dry land.

MOVING OUT OF YOUR COMFORT ZONE

By faith Abraham, when called to go to a place he would later receive as his inheritance, obeyed and went, even though he did not know where he was going. By faith he made his home in the promised land like a stranger in a foreign country.
HEBREWS 11:8-9

Remember taking swimming lessons as a kid? Perhaps you were in a pool, with the shallow and deep ends clearly marked. Ropes marked off lanes and teachers stood by, guiding and instructing you. They told you how to kick, how to breathe and how to move your arms for maximum efficiency. Pretty soon, you knew just how many strokes it took to get from one end to the other. You felt comfortable even in the deep end.

But now, you've outgrown the lessons and the safety of the pool. You are swimming in uncharted waters, experimenting with the best strokes, the most interesting direction, trying to move forward and stay safe at the same time. This is not necessarily comfortable. But you are expressing your faith in God by simply getting wet.

When you take that step out of your comfort zone to follow God in faith, it can feel like you're all alone. But you aren't the first one to make a choice to follow God, even when it is really tough. Even as far back as Moses and Abraham, people were giving up their security and comfort to follow God into deep waters, and into a more glorious future!

By faith Moses, when he had grown up, refused to be known as the son of Pharaoh's daughter. He chose to be mistreated along with the people of God rather than to enjoy the pleasures of sin for a short time. He regarded disgrace for the sake of Christ as of greater value than the treasures of Egypt, because he was looking ahead to his reward. HEBREWS 11:24-26

GOD'S GENTLE (AND NOT SO GENTLE) TESTS OF FAITH

"When you pass through the waters, I will be with you; And when you pass through the rivers, they will not sweep over you," says the Lord.

ISAIAH 43:2

Do you remember hearing the story of Jonah and the whale for the first time? As a kid, you might have imagined what it was like in that cavernous, dark and smelly whale. Perhaps you imagined what you would do if you were swallowed.

It's easy to get swallowed by a "whale" of a situation or a problem. We can get swallowed up in work, in achievements, in perfectionism, or in trying to do everything. And after we are swallowed, like Jonah, we can get spit out again, often to sink in deep water. But remember how the story of Jonah ended?

"Go to the great city of Nineveh and preach against it, because its wickedness has come up before me," said the LORD.

But Jonah ran away from the LORD and headed for Tarshish. He went down to Joppa, where he found a ship bound for that port. After paying the fare, he went aboard and sailed for Tarshish to flee from the LORD. Then the LORD sent a great wind on the sea, and such a violent storm arose that the ship threatened to break up. ...

The sea was getting rougher and rougher. So [the sailors] asked [Jonah], "What should we do to you to make the sea calm down for us?"

"Pick me up and throw me into the sea," he replied, "and it will become calm. I know that it is my fault that this great storm has come upon you." ...

Then they took Jonah and threw him overboard, and the raging sea grew calm. At this the men greatly feared the LORD, and they offered a sacrifice to the LORD and made vows to him. But the LORD provided a great fish to swallow Jonah, and Jonah was inside the fish three days and three nights. ...

From inside the fish Jonah prayed to the LORD his God. He said: "In my distress I called to the LORD, and he answered me. From the depths of the grave I called for help, and you listened to my cry. You hurled me into the deep, into the very heart of the seas, and the currents swirled about me; all your waves and breakers swept over me. I said, 'I have been banished from your sight; yet I will look again toward your holy temple.' The engulfing waters threatened me, the deep surrounded me; seaweed was wrapped around my head. ... But I, with a song of thanksgiving, will sacrifice to you. What I have vowed I will make good. Salvation comes from the LORD."

And the LORD commanded the fish,
and it vomited Jonah onto dry land.
JONAH 1:2—4, 11-12, 15-17; 2:1-5, 9-10

WALKING ON WATER: KEEPING YOUR EYES ON JESUS

During the fourth watch of the night Jesus went out to [the disciples], walking on the lake. When the disciples saw him walking on the lake, they were terrified. "It's a ghost," they said and cried out in fear.

But Jesus immediately said to them: "Take courage. It is I. Don't be afraid."

"Lord, if it is you," Peter replied, "tell me to come to you on the water."

"Come," he said. Then Peter got down out of the boat, walked on the water and came toward Jesus. But when he saw the wind, he was afraid and, beginning to sink, cried out, "Lord, save me!"

Immediately Jesus reached out his hand and caught him.
"You of little faith," he said, "why did you doubt?" And when they climbed into the boat, the wind died down.

Then those who were in the boat worshiped him, saying, "Truly you are the Son of God." MATTHEW 14:25-33

The Bible is, among other things, a list of unforgettable walks. Perhaps the most unforgettable walk was taken by Peter the day he got out of a boat and walked on the water. It was unforgettable not so much because of where he was walking, as what he was walking on and with whom he was walking. I think when Peter went treading on the waves he was experiencing walking at its finest.

Put yourself in Peter's place for a moment. You have a sudden insight into what Jesus is doing—the Lord is passing by. He's inviting you to go on the adventure of your life. But at the same time, you're scared to death. What would you choose—the water or the boat?

The water is rough. The waves are high. There's a storm out there. But if you don't get out of the boat, there's a certainty that you will never walk on water.

Water-walking requires not only the courage to take a risk, but also the wisdom to discern a call. God's method for growing a deep, adventuresome faith in us is by asking us to get out of the boat. God uses real-world challenges to develop our ability to trust in him.

I believe there are many good reasons to get out of the boat. But there is one that trumps them all: The water is where Jesus is. The water may be dark, wet and dangerous. But Jesus is not in the boat. JOHN ORTBERG

EVERY DAY, IN SO MANY WAYS, YOU ARE GETTING OUT OF THE BOAT. JUST BEING ALIVE IN THIS FAST-PACED, CHALLENGING WORLD REQUIRES FAITH AND COURAGE. OFTEN, WE DON'T RECOGNIZE OUR OWN COURAGE, OUR EVERYDAY ACTS OF FAITH.

NOTICE TODAY HOW OFTEN YOU ARE OUT OF THE BOAT. MAYBE YOU SPEAK OUT IN A MEETING. MAYBE YOU MAKE TIME TO GO TO THE GYM, WHEN YOU REALLY WANT TO GO EAT DINNER WITH FRIENDS. MAYBE YOU SEND AN EMAIL OR NOTE TO SOMEONE WHO NEEDS A LITTLE SUPPORT.

EACH PERSON'S EXPERIENCE "IN THE WATER" IS UNIQUE. EVERY TIME YOU VENTURE OUT OF THE BOAT, YOU GET CLOSER TO GOD. YOU GET CLOSER TO YOUR PURPOSE IN THIS LIFE.

In many ways, life is like running a wild river in a canoe. It has its slow spells, its threatening spurts, its seat-of-the-pants thrills, its waterfalls, its tragedies. It keeps rushing by—sometimes at a roar, sometimes at a whisper—and if you're not careful you can get tossed around like a cork and go straight to the bottom. Or you can follow the guides and the navigational charts and keep straight on course. You'll still go through the waterfalls and rapids, but you'll be on top of the water. S. RICKLY CHRISTIAN

WE WILL NO LONGER BE INFANTS,

tossed back and forth by the waves
and blown here and there
by every wind of teaching and by the cunning
and craftiness of men in their deceitful scheming.
Instead, speaking the truth in love,
we will in all things grow up into him
who is the Head, that is, Christ.

EPHESIANS 4:14-15

THE MEADOW

Meadows are wonderful places. They are full of flowers, warm grass, and plenty of wide-open space. A meadow is the perfect place to stop and rest, as it is free of the dangers you might encounter in the woods or on the mountain cliffs. It is a refuge, a place to slow down and recharge. A rain shower may cloud the skies now and then, but it is always a gentle rain that brings even more flowers to bloom and leaves the meadow smelling sweet and new.

The meadows in our lives are pastoral places of renewal and gentle respite from the "loud-hard-bright-fast" pace of life. In the meadow, you can use the soft, warm earth for a pillow, the lilting breeze for a song, the wispy clouds as your playmates. You can snooze or you can choose to lie awake. You can just be.

As you struggle on your journey of life across the deserts, through the jungles, over the mountains, and deep into the oceans, keep watch for the meadows, God's small green pastures. In the meadows, you can be with Him, the Lord, the giver of rest, the medicine for the soul, the source of eternal strength.

Re-Charging and Re-Focusing

A heart at peace
gives life to the body
PROVERBS 14:30

ife can drain us of our energy. It can confuse our sense of what is right and what is true. But there is a way to re-charge and to clear away the doubts. Focus on God, not with a great effort of concentration, but in quiet and stillness. He will give you strength and make clear His will for you.

❖

Why bother with church? My life is so hectic already that attending Sunday services is just another item on my pressure-cooker list of things to do. I've got a ton of work to do, bills to organize and pay, my place is a mess and needs cleaning, the oil in my car needs to be changed, and my friends think I am ignoring them. I don't think my schedule can take any additional strain at this point.

Do I really need church? Why?

I need church because it is a retreat.

When I get so busy that I have no time for church, then I'm simply too busy. It may be just another item on my "Things to Do" list, but it's one of the most important because it gives me time to stop, gather my perspective, reflect on the coming week, and to "be still" and meditate on God.

It's a time to ungarble my mind, restring my nerves, and calm my churning stomach. Church is a place to realign priorities, to worship God, and celebrate Christ's empty tomb. Celebrate—yes, that's the word. By no means should church be Dullsville.

In the first chapter of Genesis, the Bible details how, in six days, God created everything from cotton-candy clouds, snails, and monster surf at Sunset Beach, to the whiskered walrus, Venus fly trap, and lightning bolts. And on the seventh day he took a breather: "God blessed the seventh day and made it holy, because on it he rested from all the work of creating that he had done."

Jesus often did the same by retreating with his disciples to a sanctuary, a hiding place, where they could release their heavy loads of anxiety, strengthen their slender threads of patience and, most of all, remember their heavenly Father. As head of the church, Jesus Christ has called for us to take weekly breathers—to rest up, to celebrate ... and to remember. S. RICKLY CHRISTIAN

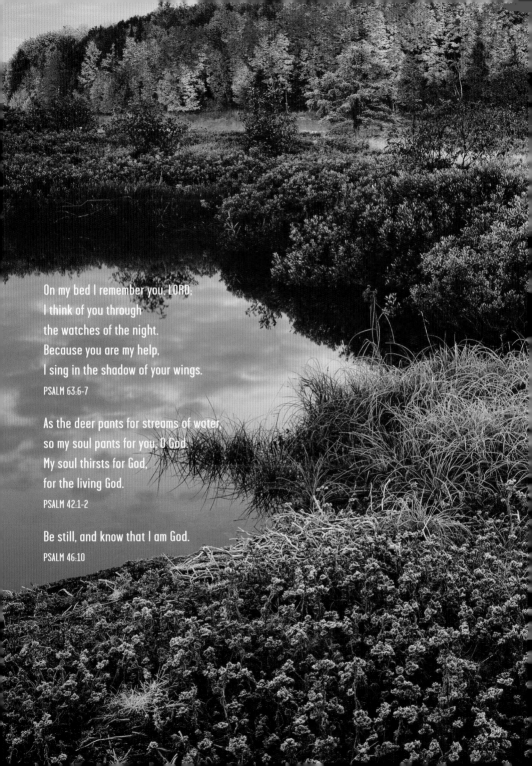

On my bed I remember you, LORD;
I think of you through
the watches of the night.
Because you are my help,
I sing in the shadow of your wings.

PSALM 63:6-7

As the deer pants for streams of water,
so my soul pants for you, O God.
My soul thirsts for God,
for the living God.

PSALM 42:1-2

Be still, and know that I am God.

PSALM 46:10

Warm Grass For A Pillow: Finding A Place Of Rest

There remains... a Sabbath-rest for the people of God; for anyone who enters God's rest also rests from his own work, just as God did from his. Let us, therefore, make every effort to enter that rest. –HEBREWS 4:9-11

Rest is experienced through diligent effort and vigilance. It seems contradictory, doesn't it? The writer of Hebrews is not at odds with himself, nor is he in conflict with the biblical principle of rest. Rather he is prescribing the exact remedy for enjoying the abundant Christian life in an entirely new dimension.

You are to rest from trying to make yourself acceptable to God. If you have accepted Christ as Savior, you are as righteous and acceptable in God's eyes today as you will be when you enter his very presence in heaven. God treats you today and forever according to the merits and mediation of the Cross, not your behavior. You are already pleasing God. You are already

holy and blameless in his eyes. Your actions may not always measure up to your identity, but you are a child of God forever. You can cease from any works of self-righteousness.

Living and working in the strength and power of your talents and abilities will only take you so far. It is a long, uphill climb that leads to eventual exhaustion and burnout. But living according to the Spirit will bring you into the green pastures and beside the still waters of the Good Shepherd. "For it is God who works in you to will and to act according to his good purpose" (Philippians 2:13). That takes the strain off, doesn't it? That infuses the very power of God into your every thought, word, and deed. God is responsible for you. He saved you. He began a good work in you. He will complete it. Surely you are to obey, but you have the power of God to accomplish all that he has planned for your life.

Enter the rest of God by placing your trust in the finished work of the Cross. Commit your way to him. This is the way of success, endurance, and cherished rest for your innermost being. It is the rest of confident faith in the faithfulness of God. CHARLES STANLEY

We would be better Christians if we spent more time alone, and we would actually accomplish more if we attempted less and spent more time in isolation and quiet waiting upon God. The world has become too much a part of us, and we are afflicted with the idea that we are not accomplishing anything unless we are always busily running back and forth.

In these hectic days, we should often give our mind a "Sunday"—a time in which it will do no work but instead will simply be still, look heavenward and spread itself before the Lord … allowing itself to be soaked with the moisture of the dew of heaven. We should have intervals of time when we do nothing, think nothing, and plan nothing but simply lie on the green lap of

IT'S OKAY TO SLOW DOWN

Jesus said, "Come
to me, all you who are
weary and burdened,
and I will give you rest.
Take my yoke upon you
and learn from me,
for I am gentle and
humble in heart, and
you will find rest
for your souls. For my
yoke is easy and my
burden is light."
MATTHEW 11:28-30

(T)ime spent resting, slowing down, is not lost time. People living in cities today would do well to follow the example of Isaac who "went out to the field ... to meditate" (Genesis 24:63). As often as possible it is good to visit the fields of the countryside, away from the hustle and bustle of the city. After having grown weary from the heat and noise of the city, communion with nature is very refreshing and will bring a calming, healing influence. A hike across a meadow sprinkled with daisies will purge you of the impurities of life and will cause your heart to beat with new joy and hope. L. B. COWMAN

As Jesus and his disciples were on their way, he came to a village where a woman named Martha opened her home to him. She had a sister called Mary, who sat at the Lord's feet listening to what he said. But Martha was distracted by all the preparations that had to be made. She came to him and asked, "Lord, don't you care that my sister has left me to do the work by myself? Tell her to help me!"

"Martha, Martha," the Lord answered, "you are worried and upset about many things, but only one thing is needed. Mary has chosen what is better, and it will not be taken away from her." LUKE 10:38-42

ONE OF THE THINGS I FIND FASCINATING ABOUT GOD'S CREATION IS THE WAY HE SEEMS TO TEMPER THE NEGATIVE ENVIRONMENTAL ELEMENTS WITH CORRESPONDING POSITIVE ONES. FOR INSTANCE, WITHOUT THE NEARLY CEASELESS RAINS OF THE NORTHWEST, NO INCOMPARABLY GREEN SCENERY WOULD GREET THE EYE FROM ALL DIRECTIONS. GOD'S CREATIVE STYLE ENSURES THAT SOMETHING WONDERFUL WILL OFFSET SOMETHING LESS THAN WONDERFUL. IN EVERYTHING GOD SEEMS SO BALANCED. I LOVE THAT ABOUT HIM. MARILYN MEBERG

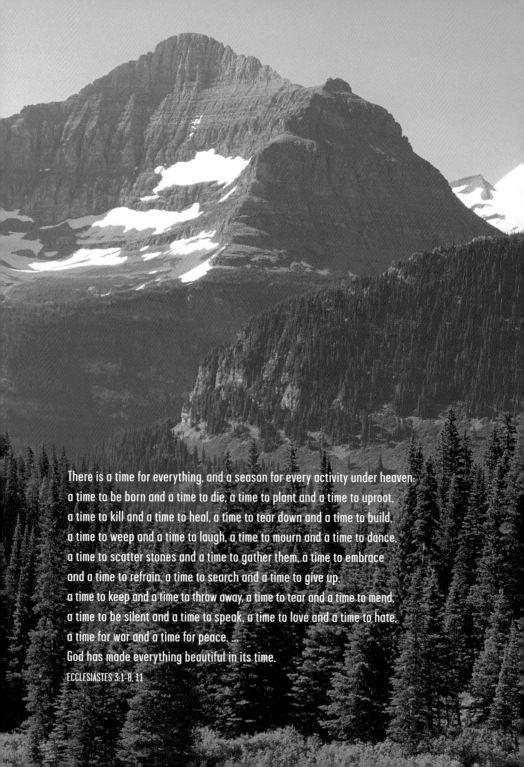

There is a time for everything, and a season for every activity under heaven:
a time to be born and a time to die, a time to plant and a time to uproot,
a time to kill and a time to heal, a time to tear down and a time to build,
a time to weep and a time to laugh, a time to mourn and a time to dance,
a time to scatter stones and a time to gather them, a time to embrace
and a time to refrain, a time to search and a time to give up,
a time to keep and a time to throw away, a time to tear and a time to mend,
a time to be silent and a time to speak, a time to love and a time to hate,
a time for war and a time for peace. ...
God has made everything beautiful in its time.

ECCLESIASTES 3:1-8, 11

MAKING A HABIT OF QUIET TIME WITH GOD

The meadow of rest, reflection, and renewal is a place to re-focus, step back, and take a broader view.

❖

It is important, of course, to be familiar with all of the Bible. Sometimes you will need to read broadly, but in reading for transformation you will need to go slowly. You can't meditate quickly. There is no course in speed-meditation.

Some time ago, I set a goal of praying through the Psalms, one psalm a day. Each day that I could check one off the list, I was one step closer to the goal. This meant I never wanted to get stuck on one psalm for two days in a row. It was as if God had a big chart on the refrigerator in heaven, and each time I made it through a psalm, I got a gold star. Naturally, this sabotaged God's real purpose. He wanted to speak to me, to renew me. What I had failed to realize was that if God is using one psalm, or even one word to do so, my job is to stick with it as long as it takes until I've learned what I need to learn. Your goal should not be for you to get through the Scripture. The goal is to get the Scriptures through you.

JOHN ORTBERG

OUT IN THE FIELDS WITH GOD

The little cares that fretted me
I lost them yesterday,
Among the fields above the sea,
Among the winds at play,
Among the lowing of the herds,
The rustling of the trees,
Among the singing of the birds,
The humming of the bees.

The foolish fears of what might happen,
I cast them all away
Among the clover-scented grass,
Among the new-mown hay,
Among the husking of the corn,
Where drowsy poppies nod,
Where ill thoughts die and good are born—
Out in the fields with God.

LOUISE IMOGEN GUINEY

SPACE

Space—filled with billions of stars, unknown worlds and limitless expanses, it is the last great unexplored frontier for mankind. Leaving the familiar surroundings of earth's atmosphere and launching into space takes immense amounts of energy and puts explorers in a world where even the laws of gravity seem to be turned upside down. It is full of the unknown which makes it also full of wonderful new possibilities.

Space is like your future. It stretches out before you full of the unknown and yet so full of promise. How do you know what you are supposed to do there, how do you get started on this journey, and where will this sometimes wild ride take you? Be patient with all the confusion in space and your uncertainty as a traveler. God will show you the way.

"I KNOW THE PLANS I HAVE FOR YOU," DECLARES THE LORD,"PLANS TO PROSPER YOU AND NOT TO HARM YOU, PLANS TO GIVE YOU HOPE AND A FUTURE."

JEREMIAH 29:11

What clues do you have about your purpose?

▼ If you created a "map" of your life so far, where were the places you enjoyed going?

▼ What are the things you enjoy doing?

▼ Who are the people you like to be with?

▼ If you could go back and live one day of your life over, which day would it be?

▼ What goal would you most like to achieve?

▼ As a child, what did you tell people you wanted to be when you grew up?

The answers to each of these questions hold clues to God's purpose for your life. God speaks to us through the life he gives us.

In Christ we were chosen, having been predestined according to the plan of him who works out everything in conformity with the purpose of his will. EPHESIANS 1:11

God who began a good work in you will carry it on to completion until the day of Christ Jesus. PHILIPPIANS 1:6

Commit to the Lord whatever you do, and your plans will succeed. PROVERBS 16:3

A TWO-PERSON FLIGHT CREW:
GOD LONGS TO GO WITH YOU

Here's an idea. God placed you here for companionship with him. What an idea! God longs to spend time with you! The maker of the Universe wants to be your companion! It's true! In Revelation 3:20, Jesus said, "Here I am! I stand at the door and knock. If anyone hears my voice and opens the door, I will come in and eat with him, and he with me."

God could have created the human race, started the world spinning and left us to figure things out on our own. He could have planted a little human colony on the third rock from the sun and left us floating aimlessly among the billions of stars in the universe. But he didn't. In the Bible he says over and over, "I will be with you," to Abraham, Moses, Joshua, Gideon, Solomon ... and to us.

"I am with you and will watch over you wherever you go. ... I will not leave you until I have done what I have promised you," says the Lord.
GENESIS 28:15

We say with confidence, "The Lord is my helper; I will not be afraid, what can man do to me?"
HEBREWS 13:6

Jesus said, "I will ask the Father, and he will give you another Counselor to be with you forever—the Spirit of truth."
JOHN 14:16—17

Overcoming Peer Pressure

Do not conform any longer to the pattern of this world, but be transformed by the renewing of your mind.

ROMANS 12:2

(A) black hole is an extremely dense celestial body that has been theorized to exist in the universe. The gravitational field of a black hole is so strong that, nothing, including electromagnetic radiation, can escape from it. A black hole is surrounded by a spherical boundary, called a horizon, through which light can enter but not escape; it therefore appears totally black.

Do you ever feel you're being sucked into a black hole called peer pressure? The pull is so strong, you don't know how you're going to escape. And when you build up the courage to turn on your thrusters and try with all your might to head the other way, your peers set you apart and ridicule you because you resisted the pull of sameness and insisted on being unique. You reach out to God. You're trying to be different, to live for him. Where is he now?

Black holes in the universe can be massive—each a billion times the mass of the Sun itself. The black holes of peer pressure to conform and the loneliness of trying to resist can seem to take up your whole life. You have to remember that you're not alone. God is your pilot and he will give you an escape. Your future is in God's hands—not in the black hole!

Be strong and courageous. Do not be afraid or terrified. . .for the LORD your God goes with you; he will never leave you nor forsake you. DEUTERONOMY 31:6

I am the LORD, your God, who takes hold of your right hand and says to you, Do not fear; I will help you. ISAIAH 41:13

God is our God for ever and ever; he will be our guide even to the end. PSALM 48:14

GOING WHERE NO ONE HAS GONE BEFORE: DARING TO THINK—AND ACT—BIG

How do you become bold enough to act on the big dreams God has given you for your future? Here's some advice from Dr. Ben Carson:

"If you recognize your talents, use them appropriately, and choose a field that uses those talents, you will rise to the top of your field. Think positively. Use Positive Mental Attitude. Have faith. Thinking Big means opening our horizons, reaching for new possibilities in our lives, being open to whatever God has in store for us on the road ahead.

Over the years I have urged others to give their best, to seek for excellence, and to Think Big. One day I was mulling over those two words and I worked out an acrostic for it.

T Talent: Learn to recognize and accept your God-given talents (and we all have them).

H Honest: If you're honest, you don't have to remember what you said the last time. Speaking the truth each time makes life amazingly simple.

I Insight: Listen and learn from people who have already been where you want to go.

N Nice: Be nice to people—all people. If you're nice to people, they'll be nice to you.

K Knowledge: Knowledge is the key to independent living, the key to all your dreams, hopes, and aspirations.

B Books: We develop our minds by reading, by thinking, by figuring things out for ourselves.

I In-depth learning: In-depth learners make the knowledge they acquire a part of them so they can continue to build upon that knowledge with new knowledge.

G God: Never get too big for God. Never drop God out of your life."

To learn more about your unique field of talents,

Carson recommends this exercise. Write down the answers to these questions:

▼ What have I done well in my life so far?

▼ What do I like to do that has caused others to compliment me?

▼ What do I do well and think of as fun though my friends see it as work— or as a boring activity?

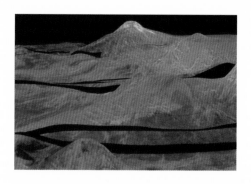

CLOSE YOUR EYES AND THINK ABOUT YOUR WORLD.
TAKE A COUPLE OF MINUTES TO REALLY PICTURE
IT IN YOUR IMAGINATION. DOES IT LOOK ANYTHING
LIKE SCENES IN A "STAR WARS" MOVIE, FULL OF
STRANGE CREATURES AND HIDDEN DANGERS?
DO YOU NEED COURAGE JUST TO STEP OUT YOUR
DOOR EACH MORNING? DOES A SPACE WEAPON
SEEM NECESSARY FOR SURVIVAL?

In your life, you will encounter characters who not only try to destroy you but also steal your stuff. Are there Space Invaders in your life who try to get ahead of you by cheating? How about two-headed monsters with a different and contradictory message coming out of each mouth?

Bob Briner wrote, "Jesus said it clearly, Christians are strangers and aliens in this world. They belong to another kingdom. They may be IN the world, but they are not OF the world."

As you debate whether to take your shuttle out of the Mother Ship to explore remote galaxies, remember that you're not leaving God's kingdom. He is with you when you are surrounded by strange creatures you don't understand and in galaxies you've never explored. Others may view you as alien, but you belong to God.

Jesus said, "If you belonged to the world, it would love you as its own. As it is, you do not belong to the world, but I have chosen you out of the world." JOHN 15:19

All these people [Abraham, Isaac, Jacob, Noah and Enoch] were still living by faith when they died. ...
They admitted that they were aliens and strangers on earth.
People who say such things show that they are looking for a country of their own.
If they had been thinking of the country they had left, they would have had opportunity to return. Instead, they were longing for a better country—a heavenly one. Therefore God is not ashamed to be called their God, for he has prepared a city for them. HEBREWS 11:13-16

SHINING IN THE DARKNESS

Those who are wise will shine like the brightness of the heavens, and those who lead many to righteousness, like the stars for ever and ever.

DANIEL 12:3

W)hat would it take for you to be a star in your universe? Not a celebrity, nor someone who has succeeded at "winning," but a shining example of God's love? Are you willing to put forth the effort it takes to be such a star?

Christian music artist Steven Curtis Chapman talks about stardom in his book, *Speechless*: "A few CDs, hundreds of concerts and thousands of frequent flyer miles later, I found myself wondering how my own spiritual pulse is. For quite a while I had become increasingly overwhelmed by the mounting pressure and pulls associated with the success of an expanding career. 'Lord, help me in the whirlwind of all this stuff. I feel like I'm losing something vital.'"

Have you become enmeshed in a universe of "stuff," trying to be more, know more, make more? What have you lost? What have you gained? All it takes to be a true star is to give yourself to Jesus. His power will make you a shining star in the darkness of the universe.

Here's what God's Word says about becoming a star:

Everyone born of God overcomes the world. This is the victory
that has overcome the world, even our faith. Who is it that overcomes the world?
Only he who believes that Jesus is the Son of God. 1 JOHN 5:4-5

Become blameless and pure, children of God without fault in a crooked and depraved generation, in which you shine like stars in the universe. PHILIPPIANS 2:15

ETERNAL LIFE

You have made known to me the path of life, O Lord; you will fill me with joy in your presence, with eternal pleasures at your right hand.

PSALM 16:11

This psalm is a song of praise to God for his promise of eternal life. But this psalm also holds the promise—one that fills the psalmist with joy—of experiencing eternity right now. Eternal life is not just a future dimension but an upward one that we experience when we know God—the living God who counsels and instructs us and makes us secure.

FROM THE COLLEGIATE DEVOTIONAL BIBLE

HEAVEN IN THE REAL WORLD

It happened one night with a tiny baby's birth
God heard creation crying and He sent heaven to earth
He is the hope, He is the peace
That will make this life complete
For every man, woman, boy and girl
Looking for heaven in the real world
Heaven has come to the real world
Heaven has come, come to the real world
He is the hope, He is the peace
Jesus is heaven, heaven in the real world.

STEVEN CURTIS CHAPMAN

YOUR WORLD STANDS BEFORE YOU, FILLED WITH LIMITLESS POSSIBILITIES, WONDERFUL PLACES TO EXPLORE, AND DECISIONS TO MAKE EVERY DAY OF YOUR LIFE.

▼ The Jungle is a tangle of decisions and choices—cut through the under-growth and drive back the snakes of greed with the strong sword of God's Word.

▼ The Mountains call you to climb, to explore, to test your limits, and to reach for the top. While you climb, don't forget to look for the beauty all around you, and give God control of your climb. He knows the best way up, and down, the mountains of life.

▼ The Desert may appear out of nowhere, burning you with its heat, and driving you to shelter with its whirling sands. In the midst of these dry times, search for the oasis of God's love. It is always there to refresh you and sustain you until you make it through.

▼ **The Woodlands** beckon you to explore with their lush vegetation and mysterious trails. Follow your guide and trust your compass, and you'll discover the relationship with God you always dreamed of.

▼ **The Prairies** open up before you, stretching to the horizon. Sometimes it seems they will never end and that you will never reach your goals. Take time to learn from the trip, and don't give up the journey, for soon you will see your God-given dreams becoming a reality.

▼ **The Waters** provide refreshment and enjoyment, but can also bring danger and fear. When you trust God and step out in faith, the waters will bring you to a new depth in your walk with Jesus.

▼ **The Meadow** is the welcome rest from traversing all the rough terrain. In this beautiful, open space, you can feel free to rest, to reflect, and to just be. Return often to the meadow to spend time with God—he will always give you strength to continue your journey.

▼ **Space**—your broad, unlimited, unknown future spreads out before you. Everything is possible. Let God pilot your ship, and you will avoid the black holes and discover a future unlike anything you ever imagined.

Real Life is here and now. Are you ready? With God on your side, you can do anything. So gear up, say goodbye to the past, and follow your Guide. He will show you the way into your Real Life!

Jesus said, "I am with you always, to the very end of the age." MATTHEW 28:20

"NO EYE HAS SEEN,

no ear has heard

no mind has conceived

what God has prepared

for those who love him."

1 CORINTHIANS 2:9

Bryson, Bill, A Walk in the Woods, © 1998 by Bill Bryson,
(New York: Broadway Books, 1998).

Carson, Benjamin, Think Big, © 1992 by Benjamin Carson, M.D.,
(Grand Rapids, MI: Zondervan, 1992).

Chapman, Steven Curtis, Speechless, © 1999 by Steven Curtis Chapman
and Scotty Smith, (Grand Rapids, MI: Zondervan, 1999).

Christian, S. Rickly, Alive 1, © 1983, 1995 by S. Rickly Christian,
(Grand Rapids, MI: Zondervan, 1995). Alive 2, © 1983, 1995 by S. Rickly Christian,
(Grand Rapids, MI: Zondervan, 1995).

Collegiate Devotional Bible, © 1998 by Zondervan (Grand Rapids,
MI: Zondervan, 1998).

Cowman, L. B., From the December 24 devotion in Streams in the Desert,
David, sixth-century Welsh saint, From the June 20 devotion in Streams in
the Desert, by L.B. Cowman, edited by James Reimann © 1997 by Zondervan,
(Grand Rapids, MI: Zondervan, 1997).

Johnson, Barbara, Patsy Clairmont, Marilyn Meberg, Luci Swindoll,
The Joyful Journey, © 1997 by Barbara Johnson, Patsy Clairmont, Marilyn Meberg,
Luci Swindoll, (Grand Rapids, MI: Zondervan, 1997).

LaHaye, Tim, Finding the Will of God in a Crazy, Mixed-Up World,
© 1989 by Tim LaHaye, (Grand Rapids, MI: Zondervan, 1989).

Leadership Bible: Leadership Principles from God's Word,
New International Version © 1998 by Zondervan,
(Grand Rapids, MI: Zondervan, 1998).

Meberg, Marilyn, Thelma Wells, Patsy Clairmont, Luci Swindoll, Sheila Walsh,
Barbara Johnson, We Brake for Joy, © 1998 Marilyn Meberg, Thelma Wells, Patsy Clairmont,
Luci Swindoll, Sheila Walsh, Barbara Johnson, (Grand Rapids, MI: Zondervan, 1998).

Nuenke, Doug, "Volcano," published in Guideposts for Teens, August/September 1999 issue.

Ortbertg, John, If You Want to Walk on Water, You've Got to Get Out of the Boat, © 2001 by John Ortberg, (Grand Rapids, MI: Zondervan, 2001)

Paup, Bryce, What's Important Now, © 1997 by Bryce Paup (Sisters, OR: Multnomah Publishers, 1997).

Stanley, Charles, A Touch of His Peace, © 1993 by Charles F. Stanley (Grand Rapids, MI: Zondervan, 1993).

Sweet, Leonard I., SoulSalsa, © 2000 by Leonard I. Sweet (Grand Rapids, MI: Zondervan, 2000).

Swindoll, Luci, Marilyn Meberg, Barbara Johnson, Patsy Clairmont, Joy Breaks, © 1997 by Luci Swindoll, Marilyn Meberg, Barbara Johnson, Patsy Clairmont, (Grand Rapids, MI: Zondervan, 1997).

Whether you turn

to the right or to the left,

your ears will hear a voice

behind you, saying,

"This is the way; walk in it."

ISAIAH 30:21